states of unitedness

poems by

J.C. SALAZAR

To all my teachers and all my students.
And to every hyphenated American who understands
the richness and the burden of it all.

Bronze Diamond Productions
805 Bomar
Houston, TX 77006
JC Salazar Publisher

Produced in The United States of America

Printed and Distributed by CreateSpace and IngramSpark

Cover and interior design by David Provolo

The Library of Congress has catalogued this edition under Salazar, JC

For information, e-mail jcsalazar.author@gmail.com
Visit the author's website: www.jcsalazarwriter.com

ISBN 978-0-9991496-3-8
     978-0-999-1496-4-5 (pbk)

Other work by J.C. Salazar:

"Of Dreams & Thorns: a Novel"

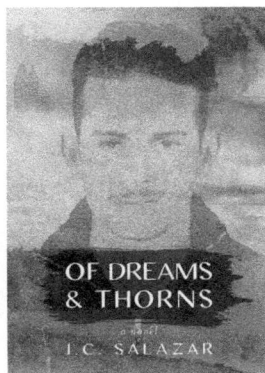

Praise for "Of Dreams & Thorns":

"Salazar does an excellent job of depicting Ramiro's transitions,
particularly during his time in Chicago as a young man; a scene
of his first visit to a supermarket is particularly vivid. The
book also effectively shows the commonalities and the subtle
differences between Mexicans and Mexican-Americans. On
the whole, the writing is strong. . . .
An often richly drawn portrait of immigration, acculturation,
and family loyalty."
— Kirkus Review

"His life journey touches on a wide range of delicate issues,
from the flaws and drawbacks of a patriarchal society to the
multifaceted implications of immigration. . . .
The author's greatest achievement is his talent to stir one
emotion after another in a bewildered reader who does not
know what to feel or expect next. . . . I recommend the book to
all those interested in reading a troublesome immigrant tale of
hardships, love, and survival."
— Official Review, OnlineBookClub.org

Contents

Section 1— Loves, Random and Real

Section 4 — Skyward Leanings

Section 5 — Tattered Earth

Section 6 — To Stave or to Hold

Foreword

I celebrate myself, and sing myself,

And what I assume you shall assume,

For every atom belonging to me as good belongs to you. . .

I harbor for good or bad, I permit to speak at every hazard,

Nature without check with original energy. . .

Perhaps I might tell more. Outlines! I plead for my brothers

and sisters.

Do you see O my brothers and sisters?

It is not chaos or death—it is form, union, plan—it is eternal

life—it is Happiness. . . .

Do I contradict myself?

Very well then I contradict myself,

(I am large, I contain multitudes.)

—Walt Whitman (1819-1892)

Walt Whitman has been the biggest influence on my poetry. I strive to make drawings with words of the essence of things, big and small. I hope that at least a few of my words might do justice to the spirit of the master American poet.

My themes consist largely of the Hispanic American experience: What it means to be Mexican-American; what is brownness? What is the immigrant experience? What diversity is there among Hispanics? What is American? Other themes include universal or international themes of humanity and humaneness, including issues of the Syrian People and other Middle Eastern areas. Some of my themes include occasion poems or tributes to certain individuals or friends. And I write of love, longing, and friendship.

I dedicate this work to all of humanity. In particular, I thank my teachers, friends, students, family, and colleagues, who have contributed in many ways to my muse and to my craft. I also want to thank you — the reader who gets it, who wants to know more, and who opens his or her mind and heart to the universality of our common human experience. To our commonality; to faith; to hope; to love!

I chose the title "states of unitedness" because my poems, overall, contain a preoccupation with our connection as human beings as well as our unitedness as citizens of America. The bonds that we have, or that we lack, to form true harmony, peace, and love define states, or degrees, if you will, of our commitment to unite and embrace our commonalities rather than let our differences define us.

These are my songs and my voice, an American voice of Mexican roots.

Section 1
Loves Random
and Real

States of Unitedness

Gradations of me;
Increments of knowledge
Of the self, and of you.
I want to hold your hand,
And you can hold my heart;
My brother, my sister,
Of my blood and marrow
Or of my thoughts alone—
No matter the bond,
Only the harmony,
The attainment of unitedness.
Give me the freedom
And I you
To grasp the widest reaches
To grow the greatest loves;
My father, my mother, my lover;
The other me, the me in other.
You of my brown-ness or my whiteness;
You of my blackness and my sands,
Oh, the infinitesimal sands,
That bind us even when apart,
Shifting, sliding, swirling
As if we mustn't ever join,
But we do.

Yes,

In gradations.

Yes yes yes yes because we must,

Because we owe it.

Each grade, each state, each place

Its own, and ours—

When we choose.

The spheres align sometimes

And perfect facets form similitude,

So hands can touch,

Arms embrace.

Or not.

At One

Solitude is my only friend;
For what is a friend if not a comfort,
To be in the presence of one's own soul?
There is no need to disguise myself,
To shirk away from my own nakedness
Reflected in the mirror on my wall
And in the greater mirror of aloneness.
The oneness with myself is welcomed
In times of lost battles with the world.
The emptiness, like endless caverns,
Beckons me to breathe deeply
The expanse of the universe.
I take the great strides to bridge the world
And span the loathsome abyss
Of every crack upon my heart
Till slowly, tenderly, one deep, long breath
At a time, I take in the mist
Of God…. and heal and grow
And dream again —
As is the fate of those at one with love.

Borrowed Rooms

I have the key to your house.
I have for years. I know its coolness
When I feel it in my pocket,
Its smoothness from its reassuring years of use.

My "borrowed" key is better worn than mine,
For I make use of it even with you gone,
As I have done this very night
To sit here and to write till you arrive.

The murky-green stained-glass window
That hangs over the clear glass of another
Makes melancholy and yet warm your room,
As is the custom of your soul to bring.

It makes me feel the comfort of the house of God;
The mansion Jesus talks of, many-roomed.
I imagine this, your house, is such a one
With splendid loving rooms of stained-glass joy.

Sometimes I Want You

It's the curve of your neck I notice first,
Savoring the smoothness,
Suppleness, or softest strength,
Of the sweeps and turns.

Or the pink of your firm lips
Beckoning, moist like youth,
And parted to a casual welcome
In their innocent natural blush.

Sometimes I'm shaken, accidentally,
By a brush of your hair,
Its innocent softness hiding brutality
In its thought-thieving turn.

On occasion, the motion of your arms,
The stride of your thigh,
The sway of your hips, the swivel
Of your waist, rivet the eye.

And I stutter midnight or morning bright
To feel your warm breath gentle
At my ear, mint or burger mist at my lips;
Or your musk from toil or store-bought.

To a Friend Away

There never is a doubt
Your skin and face and form
Are pleasing to so many;
God gave you so much more.

When you departed swiftly
With gazelle or hummingbird,
What blue skies did you rob me,
What sunshine turned to stone?

Time to finish your prodigal turn!
Time to laugh with the old company!
Think about my embrace and the more;
Turn to me, turn to home, return!

Blue Christmas

Tis the season to be jolly,
Tis the season to be true.
Everything could be so wonderful
But for the memory of you.

Oh my darling, oh my dear
To you all holiday cheer,
And if Santa grants my wish,
Your heart will be with me, here.

Old Valentine

It is the absolute familiarity
Like the daily breakfast in family,
And the needless words
When a glance says everything.
It is the infinite expressions,
Which flutter in your eyes,
Which ripple like waves upon your face,
Which speak volumes to me;
Of bonds and loves we own.
Because they come in plural,
Those layers of heart murmurs
You and I have shared for years.
The foreshadowed agony
Of imagining life empty of you,
Of the loneliness when you depart
For work or trips afar;
They, too, speak of love,
Of deep devotion and mature hearts;
Not like Romeo and Juliet,
But if you disappear, my life may end.
When I talk of one day dying,
You quickly quote Leonardo:

"You jump, I jump!"

Beauty

You are the thing of beauty above all
Who captivates my senses by your view.
Your presence in my room brings life to all,
Embarking essences to many golden shores.

There's eternity in how you hold my dreams.
There's fever in my veins to make a bond.
Your ever-innocent seduction and disdain
Become the vain of me, the thieves of life.

I, trembling hands and knees and chest,
Protest to all the nature forces of your gifts
To ask for freedom from your beauty sting
And let me hold the rein of my despair.

For that which man fears much hovers too near;
His awful stench-filled cloak of black in dregs
Making a mockery of God's struggling plan
By bringing hell to singe premature pains on me.

One moment you're the beauty of hope everlasting.
One moment you're the beauty of the poets of fame;
The force of all the ocean, the red of a fine rose.
What power has He sent, and why the mischief

When the tree says you don't see gold in me?
I feel my years of prime, my flesh yet moist,
But reaching out for glory in your stars takes life.
When you go your golden way, you leave death behind.

For when I look at you I live a lifetime;
I die a little when you walk away.

Inquisitioner

What is that thing that Spaniards used
On Jews to make them temple-free?
The wooden planks that tightened at the temples
And turning knobs squeezed till a burst
Of bone, or flesh, or brain gave its results?
That thing, and other killing vices,
That inquisitioners rejoiced to use;
The piece-meal torture chamber for each part,
That stops the breath enough to prolong pain?
How did that thing capture the deepest
Chamber of my convulsing breast,
To sit there, now for hours, now for days?
—Take it away! Take it away!

Flight with Icarus

How long can I avoid the world?
How long can passion last in this dark brew,
That knows no bounds in its almighty
Spirits that do naught but intoxicate my clay?
If passions take my flights to paths
With those like Icarus, foolishly vain,
And drinking of this sends me to harm's way,
Traversing, here a road of Eros' deadly arrows,
There a contagion like a plague of Rome,
Why thirst I more and deeper for this thing
When it hurls me prostrate to the world,
And lets it chew on me and then …. at bay?

Friend

Who is the Archangel Gabriel?
I do not know such a one,
But I know protector angel
Who's perched on my heart alight.

Like a Zephyr, winged and lovely,
Looking out for all my good,
He has come to take possession
Of my dreams and bring me truth.

The touch of his manly limb,
The rare privilege come so near;
Yet I fear this 'lectric power
Will singe all terrestrial wings.

He cannot be blamed for shining
Through warm, honey, cosmic eyes,
Nor can beauty help but thriving
On dew lips and tawny lines.

This prince of heavenly motions
Makes my door resplendent light;
Wise, athletic, witty, knowing,
Makes immortal notions mine.

My friend, Angel, sweet and striking,
Not the famous Heaven-bright;
Oneness, bronz-ed, wing-ed, you,
Fly me there my friend, anon!

But How Can I compare?

Shall I compare you to October's gold?
You are of grander splendor and more rare.
Or shall I crave you like a gourmet treat?
You tantalize me more and nourish better.

Shall I embrace you like a breeze of Spring?
Your tempers refresh more a thousand times.
Shall I find in the sun your flaming heart?
Your eyes contain more beauty and more stars.

If I should seek you out in fine Parisian scents,
No lotion can compete with your sweet flesh.
No nightingale, flute, or symphony can woo
Like each small or great melody you speak.

For as I probe your depths containing joy and folly,
I radar-locked find all of you my joy, my godly.

True Valentine

There's a light containing flecks of all the stars.
It shines like tranquil lakes alive with joy.
For all its might it fends off all vainglory
To stand like angel guarding God's own door.
Such have I found to bear this trudging road
To make sense of the backbone of true love.
And although glamour's missing from so rich a store
No Vegas neon or Great White Way shines more.

Stirrings

You win! I am trapped.
Every limb and turn of you
Holds my heart in torture chair.

Your fine arms, tamarind-hued,
Fleshy and firm, carry every motion
Like a bronze touched by the gods.

Your artisan-made eyes
Carry far greater eminence
Than festive golden skies!

Your lips of plum and roses
Turn such petals to shame;
Gazelles have not the impact
Your sinewed neck portrays.

Your tapering at the waist and thighs
And the growth there, and musk,
Beckon like rushing rapids
And hot springs.

Oh, joy to navigate the charts
That such starry poles command,
And black and flamed the abyss
To be kept so away!

You seduce like a poem ready ever to come,
But like a poem lacking its soul,
You never satisfy!

Uncontainable

When you said to me tonight
How much you enjoyed dinner,
I wanted to say — or beg —
"Can we do it every night?"

When you said that you'd be honored
If I wrote my verse to you,
I wanted to know, my darling,
"Can I say I love you, too?"

When I hear you say you need thus
Or you would like to do that,
I want to be there to give you
Everything in every way!

When I was away in New York,
Feeling lonely without you,
I confess I knew a teardrop
Desperate wanting your embrace.

As I saw one thousand marvels
In the greatest town on earth,
Every trinket that I purchased
Was imagined first was yours.

When you told me that you liked me,
Or that somehow I inspired,
I could not contain my fantasy
That you at my side would hover.

When you said you'd like to see
What I'd written by your Muse,
I shuttered in fear you'd think
My revelation too fierce.

A Friend Lost

He was there when I returned
My happy, happy friend
Asking what I'd seen in Paris
When I was away.

He was looking like an icon
In a Russian candled shrine
His golden-brown face glowing
Eyes of galaxies alight.

It was the last time I saw him,
To hold sway in lovely gaze,
For it's been ten years and more
Since those carefree days.

He has spent some years in Gotham
And in Cambridge a few more,
He has followed Madam Curry
And DeBakey's gilded lore.

From two continents away
On occasion we did write
Though our hearts seemed much the cooler
On e-mail or chats on-line.

The other evening while strolling
In the park in cool of fall
As the blue birds flew above me,
I sent my friend one last call.

Now I see from great advantage
My friend greeting birds of blue
And in joy I hear his message
It's my prayer, one so true.

Confessions

He said so much in so few words;
He said he could not stay with her.
He had not slept at all last night,
He was at war not knowing why.

He looked to me for sympathy,
For wise and tried advise,
But I could say none of my thoughts,
For failures similar had I.

He looked aghast to think he'd said
Too much, too soon, in too much dare.
He wanted I should know his soul,
But I could show no such resolve.

He saw in me more than he knew —
That my own eyes could speak so true;
That I refused to touch his soul
For fear neither of us could grow.

He said so much to me, my friend
When he the lovely maiden spurned.
He thought I knew his reasons vain.
Not he nor I could say the more.

And as my heart in ashes crumbles,
For helping motion frozen null,
I held his hand for just a moment longer,
My caution dissipating... stumbling.

Eclipse

You are the body Electric;
The form all the Cosmos adores,
Your every slope softest velvet,
Your every limb purest gold—
That mettle the envy of sculptors—
Yet graceful and swift every step
In 'lectric, astounding, most glorious
Undraped — every splendor to sun.
But if we're eternally driven
To modesty, shame, and facade,
Then all of the finery layers
I shall search the world through for you.
I'll secure rainbowed cottons and satins,
Softest leathers and pliable yarns,
And other adornments and such
That between the sparks of your eyes
And the vestments that eclipse your treasures,
So much beauty multiplied may blind.

Lover

And if I love you
It must be to the bone.
And I shall find in love nothing abhored.
And in my passion I shall know your sweat
As sweet as honey.
And what in any other heart, unlighted,
Might be a stench, or noise, or curse,
In yours, my love, it shall be aphrodisiacal.
How close to God this love reveals we are.

Mexican Love Song

Will you leave?

Will you walk out and stay away. . .

Forever?

Despite what you know of love,

Of my love;

Of the things I've done for you?

Can you leave?

Though I am yours

Like a faithful dog of years?

Do you have a fate elsewhere,

In the arms and bosoms

Of new ferment,

Where the perfumes of deep oceans

And unruly forests merge?

Where your giggle of "my lord"

Will not be mine?

And our embrace will dissipate

Like one reflected on a pond?

And should you return? . . .

You will find me sad, my love,

And angry . . .

And I will love you.

Will you leave?

Will you devalue all my inner spark

That melted hearts to forge a heart for you?

Can you be sure . . .

My wretched heart will endure

Till you return?

Desert Angel

He was a dark imposing angel —
Not the hues of Satan or that underworld,
But brown unlike cherubic blond.
He took my breath away upon our meeting
When those amazing Arabian stars
That shine in his eyes and in his smile
Turned to me like my blood,
Those eyes of ever-lasting radiance
In their oversized brown and singular orbs.
How to avoid the slippery path
Of his innocent precipice? The lure of so much
Mystery and life; the lure.... the lure.
The eagerness with which he reached
For me with grandness and with need
Awoke the needful, primal Pater
And the friend; awoke like clanging
Bells long dormant dreams, long ago
Boxed up serendipity.
He wore all the temptations
Of his fashion and the exquisite symmetry
Of God's rare beauty, the sinewy
Limbs, the graceful, muscled neck,
The ebony of his ever-sprouting
Tresses like the gift of Sampson

On balanced head and tawny cheek,
Ever announcing to the world his life,
Fertility, unstoppable and pure.
No, this was not the angel for the Pope,
But angel nonetheless, the Michaelangelo
Regret, bronzed and clumsy like his youth;
No Arabian everyman for sure,
But like the ancient land of his forebears,
The statuesque and Herculean
Nomadic angel. And with the mighty
Force of desert winds he raptured
Me with the wide span of his ebony wings,
Then spread and flew away.

Section 2
Tributes

Requiem to Selena

(On the occasion of the death of Tejano music star Selena)

"The queen," they call you,
Or "Princess!"
Tejano royalty.
Your throne a performing stage,
Your scepters microphones,
Your scroll a dancing song,
Your edicts love and joy.

Brown womanhood star, you;
Prime femme, adored to fatality.
What fatal kiss
The Cosmos you could not deny?
How swiftly did eternity
Recognize your worth
To seed new happy galaxy.

One star was pitiable inept
To bear the name Selena,
I suppose. A galaxy alone,
Some million stars,
Could live by the fire in your light.

But wretched Fate,

The cousin of Eternity,
Should have intervened
On our behalf.
Why give a hungry babe
A teat for a brief moment
Only to snatch it quick away?

The earthbound, lost and feeble,
Mourn aloud our loss,
Like so many dogs
Howling at the moon
Inconsolable, deep,
And Haunting wails.

They make this Lenten beauty
Brighter with a million lights
In noonday highways for your glory;
And equal glow surrounds
Their yellow bands of silk
About their humble cars
As they sojourn and pray
For your new Journey.

Your beaten, faithful subjects
Care not for Nature's plan,
"There are so many other queens,
Of peoples who have many.
Why take the only one we have?"

Selena,
Lovely angel-siren
Of turgid Tejano waves;
Brown royalty, our queen;
The firmament's new glow,
Envoy your new celestial powers
And make our salty sorrow
Gold!

Song to Selena

(Second perspective on the occasion of Selena's death at the hands of her fan club president)

I lost my Selena to bullets and hate.
Her cold grave now sits by Tejano sea.
Ten thousand white roses adorn her new bed,
And thousands of poems were writ that day.

In a sepulcher by the sea she lies.
The cool Corpus Christi breeze the lullaby
For my darling, my queen, my bride.
O, how it hurts to have said goodbye!

So tender, so lovely a sight to behold,
The world danced 'round her enthralled.
But evil lurked behind her traitor's home;
Her madwoman confidant carried doom.

In that tomb on the green by the sea,
Lie my hopes, my joys, my dreams,
For my lady sleeps in beauty eternally,
Great as an angel, forever apart from me.

She's radiant in her own purple gown
That she wears like the saints' holy robes,
There, in her South Texas Pantheon-home,
Whose stone doors keep me out, and cold.

O, how it hurts to have said goodbye
To my darling Selena, my bride!
How it tears my heart to walk all alone
Without music or queen, forlorn!

Upon Her Daddy's Death

As I watched the prelude to the silent sobs,
The leaves of plastic schefflera,
Ignoring the dimness of the cluttered room,
Silently sprawled
Like the outlines of a spider's web
Sketched generously on a plant,
In a corner of the family room
No longer of the family.

I watched the sofa, overstuffed
And faded, a purple squeezed of life,
Silent, solemn, stretched across the room,
As the muffled whiteness
Of draped paintings
Blindly, bluntly stared.

I knew her attic memories
Of her child's mind's laughter
And hide-and-go-seek only intensified
The tight-wet sorrow
Of her gray-green eyes
Run dry and red.

The chiffon of her black shawl,
Pellucid, nagged
At the almost chalk white hand
That struggled to repress,
At the tremulous lips, a howl of pain,
Strong and deep, from depths
She thought impossible of her heart.

I fumbled for the words to say to daddy's girl
No more, yet in the darkness
Where I knew she'd hide,
I sat and hid from her
And with her.
And cried.

In the parlor,
I dared not smile with the roses,
The orchids and carnations,
Long needy of attention.
I did not interfere with the purpose of the tears.
I let sympathy cards go unread.

Quisiera

Quisiera que todo el fuego que me quema
Fuese simplemente por tu piel morena;
O que fuese por tu perfume y su lema
Cuando te rosan mis labios en la arena.
Quisiera que solo mis partes ardientes
Sintieran la ausencia de tus firmes carnes;
O que mi pasion se mantuviera en lentes
Cuando sueles pasar por las tardes.
Pero no lo es asi, ya lo estoy entendiendo.
Porque nada tiene que ver con tus curvas
Este canto que escucho, de nuevo sintiendo,
Como por primera vez, tu me turbas.
Y hoy extraño hasta tu necedad, amor;
Tu alma me enciende con tanto clamor!

Maria Del Pilar

(Poem for my friend on the occasion of
her mother's memorial service)

I have a story to tell,
About a fair lady, much refined and great.
Our moments together were negligible
Alas, precious things are like that.
She hailed from a land of splendor,
The Spain of an era gone by,
Where the arts of romance and beauty
Balance out all devotion and faith.
When you ask her friends who's the fairest,
It's no doubt, Maria del Pilar.

What role could she best send to greatness
The mother, the wife, the grandma?
She deftly managed all these
But the wife outshines them all.
For her love story is of legends
No Juliet tragedy her love — but eternal:
Fernando and Maria Del Pilar.

Her heart and her love were expanded
When her only daughter was born.
In prescient and loving foreshadows

Maria Del Pilar she was called.
And as much as the mother was legend
Of tradition and finishing school,
The young child grew to a replica,
Yet credentialed to highest degree.

She knew all the best of her culture
In Cuba, in Spain, and then here.
But despite any hardships of migrants
She provided her family strengths.
Maria's family's dome was all treasures:
Each knick knack and art piece a gem,
And feathers arrayed in all manner
Combined with her porcelain pieces
Precious signatures of hers.

Maria was her own kind of artwork
Of graciousness beyond today
She too had the porcelain qualities
In fashion, coiff, and manicure.
Her company cannot remember
A day she was dressed out of place.
Nor the charity work or devotion
To her Catholic based principles.

So goodbye, so soon, lovely lady.
You leave us all with a void,
But better all the lives you touched;
Indeed, Fernando, Dr. Perez-Strauss,
And Sofee, your last love and pride;

The class, the etiquette... ni hablar!
All these lofty things say...
Maria Del Pilar!

Josue

Allow me to tell you a story
About a beautiful boy named Josue.
He barely knew life or its rules,
For what life can eleven years pack?

Josue lived in "Northside," a pocket
Of Houston's sprawling tapestry
Where a typical barrio home shelters a boy,
But the rough streets can snatch him away.

So it was on the eve of a bright sunny day
In two thousand and sixteen; it was May.
Richard Guerra heard the screaming first
Out in front of his home, then he saw it:

A black man, a vagrant, pinning down a boy
"Take everything. Please don't kill me."
That's what desperate Josue shouted out;
But when Calhoun or "Detroit" saw Guerra
He bolted toward the Metro tracks.

The child panic-stricken told Guerra
"I'm all right. I just wanna go home,"
But two steps was all he could muster
Then collapsed to the ground, face first.

The good samaritan promptly gave chase, but lost.
The people united and shouted for justice.
They demanded clean up of threats all around
When the killer eluded police and all tips.

The killer was homeless, a vagrant, imbalanced
As was Carlos who gave testimony in vain.
The vigils, the flowers; teddy bears, balloons
Only capture the love and the pain of the living,

But streets come alive every A.M. and eve
With kids bound for school and parents to work
The summer continued in sunny oblivion
While justice for children like this hit a wall.

Years later the case of our beautiful child
Lies unsolved, a second suspect absolved.
And the boy who loved people and science
The dreamer whose life was slashed short,

He who aspired to curing diseases one day;
To this fine, noble boy we owe justice.
Call him lovingly Josue Flores, if you will —
Josue Flores of Northside —
Or just plain Josue.

On My Brother's 40th Birthday

There was a time when you were just a brother
—My little brother I suppose—
Although I only saw the person there;
The one companion, my true friend.
We did not really have an age then.

But as the years wore on, and us,
We grew to know how old I was—
How old you were, or rather young.
And it's your youth that shone for me
That, be you five or fifty, I still see.

How many roads and many turns
Have parted us this far, and roads to come.
But through it all—the fog, the murk—
And despite all, there is a green belongs to us.
There is the heart of ancestry—and hearts to come!

Frida's Joy and Pain

Your brown forehead
is translucent to your mirror
and his browner face
is there,
as always the Tehuana
trapping you,
like the pain
of a cut on your flesh,
un-anesthetized.
When you wear the lace and silk of love,
well pressed and fancy,
they hide your anger well,
or expose it.
He is a blinding beacon
on your head, with black strings
that tie the heart
he cannot soothe
his violence-born scrapes
like the mirror in your brush can,
your only friend.
But your tiny white flowers lift you
almost as his kiss,
and in one hundred years,
millions of strokes from now,
a million flowers
will your glory bring.

J.C. Salazar

Snow White

(For a colleague who serves students with disabilities)

I once met a girl named Sue;
She was open, rare, and true,
And to our halls of lectures and books
She brought more than smiles and looks.

I called her Snow white, to be sure.
And in good sport and heart so pure
She would smile at my high praise
Of helping her wards as in a craze.

Through the weeks and months and more
I saw her near and far, the stuff of lore.
And throughout, my eyes always met
This Snow White and troops, the set.

Her pupils are certain no myth;
In their loyalty and love of width.
Yes, her wards how lucky to romp
For this Sue of kindness and pomp.

So the girl named Sue that I know
Sure is lovely, some say pure as snow.
And I'm richer for touching her light—
This girl named Sue, this Snow White.

Big Sister

I can't say that her mother knew it,
But her newborn baby was a flower named,
And the pretty baby, the first of her daughters,
Always carried such honor on high.
For as the years passed, not always in kindness,
As they tend to be out there,
Yes, out there in the valleys of clamorous airs,
The kind which ask much of the flesh,
But in turn make offerings of splendid skies,
And in its greenery one can see God—
To the baby Hortencia, whose name is of flower,
Also in her eyes held the gift of green.

It was just a marvel of those trodden paths
To view the young girl one more of the flowers,
And since her spring days, from all roads around,
She'd many admirers till this day.
Yes, she had inherited all the fine sculpture,
The precise graces of her mother true;
But her beauty was more than external in nature,
Of the vulgar world, of material things.
The young lass Hortencia, Tencha of her daddy,
The healthy young woman, the beauty,
Also carries treasures of calmness and light
In her soul of purity and her simple love.

Who measures the fleeting years, gluttonous,
Which take us nowhere and rob us of peace?
For the little girl suddenly a woman stood;
So quickly the wife and the mother too—
And the flower Hortencia has taken her soul
To new heights, new seeds, I would say.
She has forged an art form of her dedication,
Her discipline, and respect for home.
And as if by magic she has
In turn formed new, deeper roots,
Plants, and fresh trees.
And those great forces that have fruited thus
Also make the beauty of which I have told.

It seems all a lie that now half a century
Little has diminished the splendor of bloom,
For only so little ago I depended
On her lullabies, her compassion and care;
I would be prideful when all my buddies,
Once upon her visage would ask, "Who's she?"
For by transference, as happens in families,
I too relished in her bright elán.
That's why it's important to acknowledge
The exemplary force this spirit bestows,
And to celebrate her and congratulate us
For being all ours and for what she gives.

Section 3
Hyphens
and Browns

Hyphenated American

And the silence grew in my father
Until I disappeared. In my replacement
English voice
Nearly that of an Eliza —
The Galleria, River oaks, and me
My own Professor Higgins, the hyphen gone.
And the hyphen gone?
"Write about what you know," she said.
It echoed.
"Write about what you know; about being Mexican."
"Mexican! …"
The hyphen knocked.
"I am not Mexican. I am not one thing.
I am the universe."
The hyphen knocked loudly
In that poetry class. It was a gentle knock
At first, ever so gentle.
It grew over the years, then faded.
It never ceases to this day.
The fear, the pain, though gone,
Have their successors. The agony today
Is for the rainbows all the gold and seashores,
Green parrots, fragrant guavas, waterfalls;
All that the void still craves,
But the hyphen keeps away.

A Mexican is Made of This

A Mexican is made of song
That moves the soul to dance
With sprinkles of the laughter
That grows deep in the heart.

Add to the mixture hugs and tears
And humility galore;
There's faith and pride and valor
And a dash or two of hope.

A Mexican's a dreamer
Who holds a reservoir of jest;
Family ties come made of steel;
May tenth every mama is queen.

To make a Mexican the cosmos
Lassoed the rainbow whole.
They come in handsome brown
And yet in all the colors Angels do.

A Mexican is no delicate purebred:
A hearty hybrid, tough and free,
He springs from multi-scapes
Where Venus reigns laissez-faire.

J.C. Salazar

Spanish proud and Indian stoic
Comprise some flavor there
But unlike the hearty maize stock
The hybrid from violence comes.

Piñatas, mariachis, romantic evolution;
Catholic virgins, charro dandies
Their land a gift of paradise mosaics
And always room for childish joys.

To make a Mexican it takes much spirit,
Rainbows, bronze, backbone, butterflies.
If rainbows are in short supply,
You can always improvise.

Mestizo

Brown mestizo young man
Of smooth cinnamon skin
Do you know the fire
That you burn within?

Do you know the fire
That you burn in her
With your coffee fervor
And your cocoa soul?

Young man of the brown skin
That you wear so taut
Do you know the power
Of your bronzed heart?

Why the somber honey
In those nutmeg eyes?
Why not shine their passion
Like your Aztec thighs?

Your breath sweet and tasty
Like the maple brew
And your touch is spicy
Like a ginger stew.

Your voice is deep or tender
Like so many thoughts;
Your laughter makes giddy
Like forbidden smoke.

Brown man, young and lovely
Like the light of God,
Strong and cinnamonny,
Touch the sky!

Brown Fire

Hey, brown girl
With the cinnamon thighs,
Ample and powerful,
Pedal madly that rusty bike.

Sway your nutmeg bosoms
In breezy noonday
To market for a master
Who moves your lot.

Extend those limbs of chocolate
Graceful as a swan,
To gather listed packages,
Brush a tear aside.

Set those deep-honey pools
Of your Amazon eyes
Beyond the burnt of autumn
Perpetual to your load.

I will be there, resplendent
As coffee or dark brandy
As I have ever breathed in you
Brown girl,
Brown fire.

You In My Whiteness

White spheres like tiny snow marbles
And larger like a beach ball
All sizes but all ivory
Color absent
But the shades of whiteness
And their own shadows
In gray waning moons
And the sky behind them
Is a vast white drape
Smooth but for the caressing clouds
O how these spheres, my orbs
Of pleasure and of dreams
Find motion and complete my joy
Like bubble baths and children
Making bubbles out of ivory soap
And as I whirl about
In waves of sunny white
That moves the micro planets
How high each alabaster moon
Elevates me
As it holds your eyes and smile
White and invisible to naught
But me

Desperado

I contemplate your dainty hexagon
Of cherry wood, left behind,
Purple, pink, and gold.

It has a keyhole on its side,
And it holds your soul.

It is no mere music box, I know.
Nor can it be for needlepoint.
It must contain the sighs
And verse
From broken and robust hearts.

Family Argument

This is not about you, my Anglo friend.
Why does everything have to be about you?
Is it possible that I can celebrate myself
And not offend you
Because I left you out?
If I say that my brown brothers suffer
Or my Mestiza sisters are oppressed,
Why does that make you nervous?

You say to me,
"I see the flower in your song, but it is racist."
Racist?
I do not utter a disparaging word
Against you, my adopted family.
I paint the face of history,
Some sociological vignettes.
But I love you as everyone does.
You are loved.
Can we say the same about the Brown?

My enemy is not the White.
When my song does not embrace you,
I do not reject you.
My focus is the downtrodden.

states of unitedness

I say to them, "Stand up!"
No more groveling on your knees, man. . . woman!"
You are a piece of God, brown people!
You have the answers. I am a conduit for answers.
Use me. Use me, for you are my answer too.
I need you to be strong
Just as you need me, or want me, to fend for you.

I am ashamed that sometimes I am ashamed
Of the reticence of my people, of their misinformation.
But what is ignorance?
Everyone is ignorant about something,
Just like you, my Anglo brothers, are ignorant about the brown.
So why not learn something,
Why be so bored when I sing their old sad song?
When you bore me with your whiteness,
I am racist? What is it
When I bore you with my brownness?
Those Who Have and Those Who Want

The big man was as he should be,
Holding his dais before the gathered
Benefactors he called peers.
He stood up frank and strong
To be praised the most candid, true.
The multitude like sheep followed,

And now they smiled and now they cheered.

There was applause for him, and mirth.

Such adoration elevated him

Yet again, for he was big and made bold.

And in the crowd the leaders, basking,

Gave the cues to dialogue.

So no one could expect the dowse

Of an icy probe from one among the throng:

"Tell me, my leader, do you know,

For a year now you will not take my call?"

The big man lost the sparkle of his mouth,

The proud grin of those too-validated in their power,

As if a flabby nakedness had been exposed;

And the multitude was hushed and shifted

In discomfort for their venerable guest.

Who was this simple-minded lamb

Who took the chairman at his word and sang?

The big man answered curtly: "surely

A clerical mistake. On Monday next expect reply,"

And moved on to former comfort zones and to new call.

For too quick came an elder, tried and true,

To rescue the sir from such turpitude.

Said he, "Nay, sir, not so, not me!

Nay, sir, such views are flukes, you see."

The cue was unmistakable to the young

Would-be big men and big women alike.

The chairman, now re-composed in such a shield,
Returned to elder statesman, to the grin,
And a young lioness was called on next,
The protégé of prior elder she, and said,
"Nay sir, not fair to ask, not here!
You surely provide for me, and most, I hear."
And thus it is that kings are often spared discomfort
With uninvited shields that wannabes provide;
And thus ingénue learns the hard lessons,
That the crumbs of power are wont to teach
To the credulous who take their big men
At their word.

I Am Not Brown

I am not brown like I'm supposed to be,
Like your eyes, American, persist
On coloring me;
The brown of mud and foreign coffee,
Some suppose I should be.

I am white and dichotomous.
An American like me,
With hyphens painting brown
To label for expediency, to store
If you will, is easer to peg,
Like neatly packaged Spam.

I am not brown, the hell with that!
Jose or Juan or Pedro reminds you,
Yet they come in white and red and black,
And American just the same.

I am not brown like my friends.
My brother, it is no shame.
My brothers just the same.
Despite my country's fretting
And myopic glare

I span other worlds.
I claim my stars.
I know my stripes.
I take my tomorrows.
I know the power of my soul
Is greater than your thoughts.

The chaos in my eyes is your perception,
For white and black and brown alike
Are slaves to history's brush strokes.
Veneer-covered America,
The time is long past Crayolas.
Time to scratch the surface.

I am not brown by your definition.
My embrace of the brown is my business
And my strength lies there as much
As in my whiteness and in my red blood.

Moving to the Other Side

When he was born it was another century
Where a man left the boy much too soon
And the land made demands to survive;
It was a land of caciques and treasures denied.

It was a time and a place about family,
About mothers and fathers and blood
Sharing deep bonds and obligations,
Hardscrabble with Spanish pride.

A place where boys pitch in at work,
And their dreams were for boys of their own —
And a girl — or even three or four
Like the centuries of families before.

When he met his lady, his destiny,
Then saw his first born in her arms,
The weight of the world was in feathers
Till the land held back and hunger formed.

So his dreams turned to mythology
Of northern lands on the other side.
He heard, like his brother before him,
His children would never want there.

Amidst many tears, loving hands, tight embraces
The man and his wife said goodbye to the clan,
And grandma in sighs like the many relations,
Arms extended, saw them off to the other side.

Brownsville

Brownsville is a place in your mind—
A state ... of mind,

Where everyone is somber.
Everyone is crude.
Rudimentary notions live like petrified wood.

Fleshy adolescent girls
Grow long tresses there, to grow
To marry blocky studs.

Dusty, noisy streets not always named
Lead to paths of dearth
For old and newlywed.

Brownsville is a dwelling to avoid.
Highways lead you there;
More often, it's the brown-burnt horizons
Your mind hoards. ...

Mestizo Too (Chicano)

Metaphorically Castrated studs.
You walk around in baggy chinos
Holding your pseudo-manhood through your women,
Wherein lies the only source to balm your torture,
To fulfill your primal quest for supremacy.
Fragile manhood borne of economic slammed doors
Is all that drives you onward, for manhood must proceed,
To harden the resolve the child inevitably lost.
You know no other way to sense your journey.
Yet the princely primping that you tease her with
Deludes you into a Prima Donna and makes you insufferable.

You have buddies just like you at the drive-in
To lift you to oblivion even of your sons,
Forgetting such neglect was your undoing,
While girl-woman-Madonna-whore-wife waits
And waits and waits, knowing complaining is in vain,
And finally is made your accomplice in falling
With you into the dark abyss of violent barrio life,
You fall and she must fall with you, and your son,
Like the barrio, hurl to the precipice
Of denial of all the wrongs you petrify,
And scattering to cold winds all goodwill signs.

Machos don't play with dolls and men don't cry.

Those are your mottoes, right or wrong.

So you marry a doll and play house at will

All the while fooling everyone and fooling around.

Your studly energies diverted from your study

Quickly produce clones for validation, new ragdolls;

And the junior's a man at thirteen, desperate to prove it.

There is nothing to fear but fearful men

And as you paid the price of fear inherited

Since ten, your women, too, succumb and pay.

Generations later there is nothing to fear

But fearful men . . . and women. And children

Pay compounded price as you once did

Because fear will not be quelled with laws,

Nor the lofty sermons of the Irish priest

You only encounter at funerals and weddings.

The generations and the spirits lost are painful,

And as you wail the irreplaceable and beat your chest,

How can you reignite the guiding light?

Don't you know your devils are within?

Your devils are the hatred of your primordial parts,

Induced by centuries of blinding, wretched strife.

You have known the conqueror, rapacious and cruel.

You have known the conquered, believing and earthbound.

Can you hate the aggressor — your aggressive?
You hate the Indian for submission too, you think,
And for your racist roots, and your new racist home.

There is a vacuum in a man who dwells in hate,
Especially the self-hate of a million regrets,
Of knowing all the could-have-beens but for your mundaneness.
You know the landscape of the north has triumphed.
It suffered toil and war and blood to do the job,
So many duties to secure its destiny of opportunity.
This northern Eden has built all the golden cities
DeLeon could just imagine, or hoped some magic
Indian gods had done the work. The genocide of Indians
Be damned! The work of building the new Eden is at hand.
And work it is — violence, vision, plan, and sacrifice — work.

European dreamers learned to do the job without reproach.
Prosperity is justification if man or minister broke
A commandment or two for posterity. Their motto unspoken.
Look at the horn down south — the Pampas thrive.
There is a lot to celebrate in peace of mind,
But there's a lot to fear a self-cannibal mindset;
The grip of psycho-prison self-imposed.
Malinche tutored well Cortez's lessons to her half-breeds.

The wonder is the power of your place, your mind,
That you, like some Pavlovian trick, are blind
To the heavy racist chains you self-shackle unwittingly
Or assist in putting on although you've heard whispers
The breakout is your reach. The comfort of the familiar misery
Forces a deaf ear of you and fulfilling your failure-
Prophesies validates your starving intellect.

You made a journey for a better life
Although the road is forgotten in the shock
Of your devastated manhood, chained to play
Hard games where no rules were made by you.
The transitions gave you distance from your Edenic
Land, a distance your new name treasonous bares.
And in the land of English domination
You've found added illusions, disillusions, hate.
Your primordial self-rejection of Malinche birth
You thought you left behind has easily been wakened
To new amazing heights, to black brothers' surprise.
What's it like to walk like the dead-alive?

You know, Nosferatu had time on his side, and magic;
Unlike your measly portion, constantly robbed,
For you are gullible to beer and smoke and rum.
Sure, you have your moments, some good times.
Now and then a cousin breaks away and shines.

But you, like a paper tiger, a paper Latin-lover
Impresses who or how ... or .... why?

Beyond your petty, bloody birth you have great roots.
Your parentage claims imperial Spain, magnificent
And strong. And more. The Aztec sun and gold
And plumes are in your core. Who the mother
Or the father be of these is sure your choice alone.
Yet today this hefty pedigree you disregard
And fail at mounting the new cavalcade.
What good is life in Athens for a slave?
Why live in Rome and choose to be a plebe?

Are you God-forsaken? God does not forsake.
Would you choose to prove the Nazis right?
Your mind can take your blood to new great heights.
Why wear the dirty mantle of a half-breed
When there's the strength and purity of hybrid?
The chains are heavy, surely they must be,
But there are many weak or missing links.
Shake off the weight. It is not the bind you think!

Tigers and Cubs

The Mexican-American feels little,
Insignificant as an old century child,
Meant to be seen not heard.
Or worse,
For you are neither seen nor heard
In the mainstream corridors and echelons
Of power that make up America's face.
The despair of voicelessness
Is coupled with salty anguish
Of invisibility, American-made,
Euro-enriching, damning all others.

A two-hundred-and-fifty-year parallel
Of Anglo spiral upward,
Like a mythic beanstalk, a tiger's leap;
While mestizo spirals downward
Like frenzied misdirected winds;
Neither guided by a single wizard;
Both holding forth for promises
Of the land that nurtures Oz.

The littleness
Points to no master source.
Could it be as simple as a card

A tarot reader doles on fates?
You believe that, reinforced
By five hundred years of linear church,
Yet doubting ever-more
Newly-minted politics,
A black hand-me-down, accusing
The modern masters of your fate.

Someone yells at you, "It's not your fate!"
To no avail. You go on
Salmon-like in ferocious
Swim to your peril, but survive.
Yet, unlike the cosmic power
Of the awesome pink fish
Yours is a legacy
Of mangy dogs chasing their tails.

Some say you're at your best
When you can eat your young.
Against your will, you prepare
The prey, the browner the more taunting,
To devour your better parts,
Then rebuke the phantom-like
Leftovers, feeling little,
Vowing to change that gruesome course.

No one survives intact.

The preyed-upon predator

Survives and blames on instinct

The beige-pink-white world

Which holds little white,

Oblivious to its inheritance —

Itself an inheritance —

Of comforts and of guilts;

Enjoying the first passively;

Indignant, denying other hurts.

Silent — cowardly or misdirected —

Battles rage on;

The weaker trying hardest

And losing the more for it;

School and all its mental tools —

Seeming luxuries — slip by,

Robbing the brown of luster and command;

While the strong feel the war

Only a pesky itch and stir most

To avoid the squalid sight,

Never perceiving you a worthy foe.

Retreat from battles ever lost

To battles better won.

Your manhood and your womanhood

Alike seek victories however small.
You're never satisfied, though—
Not when you eat your young;
Not when you battle brothers;
Not when you win at love.

What struggling cub you are,
Magnificent in brown;
Needful of tenderness, yet rebuking
Embrace. Loving the stranger
— For you must always love —
You blame for your wounds,
Yet driving him away
By your distrustful, clumsy hug.
And while a cub may some day grow formidable,
Immediacy must remind you,
A cub is most beautiful
Just being a cub.

Your Own Path

There's a great cave in old Mexico, they say,
Filled with stocks of gold for the brave and true.
It is there for every man or woman like a prize
That rewards fearlessness of the one on a quest.

Regional men and women, children too,
Wear the simple cottons of forebears,
Soft sympathies, too, like their land.
And they fear the unknown of the alone.

They have long, craggy roads to travel, they know.
Over jagged hills, leafy forests, and parched plains;
Lowly mesquite shrubs and prickly cacti
Yield the meager sustenance the weary traveler craves.

Joaquin passes other jungles, dark and deep.
They beckon with breezy cheer and flowery rest.
He stops with a few coins, becoming fewer then,
Briefly, or finds canned sardines and bread at distant posts.

He looks back on years of searching like de Vaca,
Over verdant circles and long-gone good times,
Of tumultuous laughter on familiar chairs,
Of hearty and bestial pals, fleeting just the same.

He finds many rooms his, as he wishes great,
Which beg for building more and comfort store,
But bride or wife or concubine from ignorance
Help to pastiche the walls, to keep winds that must go.

Occasionally all human company withdraws
To reveal sparkling new paths, some diverge,
Some seem paved in gold as in tales of old Gringos,
Leading to a horizon he adores, or thinks it so.

Too brief they last, these heady times,
Yet slowly they extend, choosing the better paths,
For as a boy he could see the spark that so many ignored
Could be his in yonder adored window and golden shore.

The merry, earthy friends and loves awhirl
Interrupt him too soon, and to divert;
Confused that lonely paths offer such joy, he doubts;
Ambrosial bosoms tempting further pleasure-thoughts.

There are lovely brown maidens to be known,
Horses to tame and fattened cattle to rope;
Muscular lads to embrace or to duel
Beckon away from the trail to the magical road.

Gold caves alone hold no temporal guarantees
For the senses that they sorely need.
And the bars of treasure, like his many rooms
In the stately hacienda, cannot be removed.

He balances all their worths like his happy brothers would
— the carnal pleasures of sweet kisses and wine;
The ethereal pleasures of Shakesperean rhyme;
The golden abyss in the cave — rapture in solitude.
Yet the beacon of hope echoes his lonely quest
That the road he must keep is the best.

Grateful for the Work

They work.
They work hard—
Not afraid of work.
The grunt work is all theirs,
Kills them sometimes
Or maims.
Never mind promotions.
Content with digging,
Steady pay.
Bricklayer? ...too big a dream!
One hundred degrees.
No shade.
The digging doesn't end.
The work is good for food,
Good life.
Take a salt pill for the sweat.
Ignore nausea
To prove man enough.
Make the grade.
Four-fifty an hour in '74.
No slowing down.
There's laying down
Of pavement
For blue-eyed families

J.C. Salazar

Flying out.
Move despite the heat —
Heavy shovel, hot.
Pray for a breeze.
Can't go down.
Won't let down.
Grateful for the work
And the melanin.
Sub-divisions to build.
Subordination unknown.
Endure with a few jokes.
Bumpkin-class humor
For a little class
In life.
Think of her and the kids.
So many loved ones,
So must work.
High noon relief—
Bless the shady oak.
Hurry to the lunch pail.
There's love in there,
And pride.
Manhood.
To get through the day.
Loving hands made tacos.
Five A.M.

With a kiss for the day.

Three o'clock is hottest.

Where's that freckled kid?

Thank God for child's play —

Lemonade and iced-tea,

Fifty-cents a glass.

One hundred degrees.

Just two hours to go.

Thank God for Tommy.

Jimmy entrepreneur.

Their summer boss

In five years.

Grateful for the work.

Can't slow down now.

Saturdays? .... O.K.

Won't ask for overtime pay.

Grateful for the work.

Have a wife to keep.

Three kids in school to feed.

No one will go hungry.

Must work hard.

Must keep this job.

Little Paco's 12.

In 3 years he can help.

Start'em young to harden

Like hard life demands.

He's a man.
Five o'clock whistle.
Carpool to rush home.
Six-eleven handy.
Grab six-pack for ride,
60 minutes long.
Cool shower and fresh tortillas
Waiting home.
Grateful
For her work.

Section 4
Skyward Leanings

A Toy

Each child is a prize.
Too many children to supervise.
Assured safety lies inside.

Little Joey holds a gun,
Small and lying for a game.
He and Louis, Albert,
Mikey too, only two.

Cousin Jimmy's off to camp;
His room just for us,
The new toy a present,
His daddy's surprise.

First the banter,
"Bang, bang!" in pretend,
In the corner bedroom,
Grownups far away.

Moms and dads in social whirl,
Livingroom abuzz.
Middle kids learn flirting
Outside.

Children banter cowboy dreams.
TV on for guide.
Cousin Jimmy will be pleased
With his new toy gun.

Joey checks it out one more time.

Cowboy banter,
"Bang, bang!"
Mikey plays the Red.

"Bang!"

Mikey's . . . dead!

Believing

You have the power of the stars
If you can make the sleeping rooster crow,
If you can taste the wine long gone,
If you can turn cellophane into gold.
Shake off the venom and the fear.
Throw out the gossip of the lost.
Try on the garments of the sages.
Stretch out your arms onto the sky.
The world is too much with us
When we writhe in pain in vain,
When misery piles onto piles
And blinds us to great hopes.
Take in the air of yonder forests;
You have the wherewithal to do.
Caress the heart of velvet in your bosom.
Your power is believing makes it so.

Growing Pains

At him.

That strike again!

Like spilled paper on sidewalk,

or cruddy tree birthings on your car,

you strike;

you pass his portal

haughty in desperation, yours alone,

presuming supremacy yours and denied,

born of sheer will and nurtured

by self delusion,

and so you strike.

With victim's cloak

your only ticket to get near

to aim the strike

just so,

milking the last patient drop

a sympathetic can squeeze,

earning disdain

for hollow, niggling whines;

as fragile as a space shuttle

a tile piece amiss;

ignoring and revising

mentor now outgrown,

or unworn,

by your Narcissus urgings,
you strike.
How else to shake awake
the shrunken Alice
your eyes know
his sage has made?
So strike!
like a little emperor,
fearing only he can see
to your naked bone,
you must strike;
unsatisfied with simple truths,
reeling for hard-fought lies
that comfort bourgeois veneers,
you strike!
And then,
again. . . .

San Pedro 1963

You were a marvel to my child's gaze;
Edenic as my thoughts then and my voice,
Your river still pristine in its clear and rocky sprawl.
As I recall, mama milked the brown cow
While I chased yellow butterflies and hummingbirds.
What magic I saw there!— especially the women,
And their flair to wear romance.
Women, I say? — girls, really — eternal nymphs of memory now.

Their names? — Edwviges, Trinidad, and Candelaria
Appropriately archaic and obscure;
Hermelinda, Ambarina, and Cornelia —
Pure and simple as in their land of birth;
Paquita, Juvencia, and Hortencia —
Without pretense, Feminine, strong;
Ofelia, Isidra, Rafaela, Criselda —
Pretty and classic like their once-Spanish eyes.
Would-be pinup peasant girls in long, bouncy ponytails,
And bright cotton dresses, Mexican rose and tangerine,
Wearing their neatly coal-ironed waists like honor badges;
Faces of honey-cream complexion
And cheeks of Earth's own primal flowers.

Their first quickness their duty, their work;

These and their hearty mothers mowing chores.

Taking to the mill buckets of corn

Dekernelled, boiled, and cured the night before.

Weaving in twos and threes and fours

Down long dusty roads,

Lined with bushy mesquite and chaparral.

Midmorning, after drawing water with Athena-like strength;

Cooling morning waters, for all the norms of dawn:

Meals, hygiene, gardens, and tamed streets,

From the family's white-washed well, in oleander breeze.

Swift and graceful as Venus, they wound

The hemp rope, deliverer of vein-water most pure —

Neatly 'round imaginary spool, or made it

A sleeping, coiled snake like those that lie

Just beyond the orange grove that surrounds the house.

On school excursion days there was the forest,

Or what would pass for one,

Where a desert laid just the other side.

It held its rainbowed microcosm, though.

Of the wild berries — orange, red, and blue —

I never had enough!

And the anacua tree, so far away now,

Is still a lure.

Deep enough in the semi-desert jungle
Tiny fly-like bees made gray, rough-paper
Nests of miniature catacombs containing honey;
Whose sweetness was worthy of Zeus himself
And so much deity more;
Which daring lusty boys of eighteen brought home
To prove their love for hearth, and their manliness,
And to woo the maidens' hearts.

The captivating maidens, sweet and proud,
Of old San Pedro of '63.
Undisturbed by wires, tar, and pipes;
Pristine as the Nazareth of Jesus,
And in my mental stores held now —
Forever young, innocent, and bright,
They and their dreaming
Of handsome, wild-honey-bearing lads:
Pastorals more lovely and more vibrant
Than those of famous Grecian urns —
And safer from attacks from man
Or beast, or aging turns.

Foreshadow of a Funeral

I thought about your death last night
And became robot-like, all hot pain gone,
Imagining your waxen, powdered
Figure in silk-lined box, demanding tears.

Grandma's were not crocodile tears
In the old country when uncle Beto died,
And the family's many women chorused her,
Like Italian paid mourners, to prove their love.

You always complained about your children
Not caring enough to cry for you when you died
And shaming your name in death by it,
Which in life you neurotically over-prevented.

So I see your gray fancy box, half opened,
Like a prop a poor magician fumbled aside;
Fat long candles, yellowing, hold your corners.
Nostalgic visitors wail in the next room.

Your soul freed now from human, lying trappings
Forgives my almost-stranger's heart and tear,
Betraying your formerly precocious manly fears,
Gratefully forgetting egos of the carnal self.

But I pity you despite its uselessness
For you so loved romances like a Mexican baptism,
And this death, now and here, is not a show,
Not the old country's home-based pomp.

Not hot winds blowing o'er rocky, dusty streets
Where riders, like Revere, announce the loss
To all at near and far, and mourners cross
And dress in black for you as they've rehearsed.

They've come along on foot, horse, and machine —
The women first with babes and ready sobs.
Black veils, rosaries, and pots of home made stews,
Minutes after arrival of the reaper's news.

Ah, to die in a place where loss makes noise!
Your name and company made famous, yearned;
Where brother, friend, and enemy alike
Broker your place in Heaven or your peace of mind.

I am sorry it's not like you were promised,
That you could not by force of will make it so;
But that kind of father/son love was never taught
You, nor me, as you should know. Guilt is for naught.

Are you agnostic still or shall I pray?

No matter. You have the yields of other lessons:

Solemnity, care, burial, all attentive needs—

And proper occasion respect for good measure.

Section 5
Tattered Earth

Crossed Emotions on
a Springtime War

The headlines and captions blare of triumph

That is ours as presupposed for weeks;

The world is at our mercy now,

Having succumbed to capitalist might.

The promise of democracy prevails

Whether or not the practice gets fulfilled,

And as a despot in the turbulent cradle of humankind

Thumbs his nose at us, he falls.

We are the rule, we Americans, we hegemony,

And we shall use our might at last.

The tech precision, the tech of power, is launched

This week of springtime just arrived, and like

The new century with all the gadgets made for pleasure

And for power at a price, displays the war colors

And scopes like one more child's game.

The third-world dictator singled out among his peers

Is cornered like one mouse before one hundred cats;

And outside my window flowers bloom and burst

Like harmless beauty bombs for show of spring.

The flowers are called Azaleas, and I imagine

There is a woman, bright with life in the desert

Along side the Euphrates who also bears that name.

I see them and the blue sky bathed in sun,

In light of spring, in light eternal;
I see the flowers and the oblivious bees
From within the comfort of my plush apartment
In the neighborhood prohibited to most.
And I read the newspaper headlines of the victories
My armies win as I sip fresh hot coffee and savor
Buttered croissants glistening in orange marmalade.
I hear the anchors' handsome faces on TV proclaim
My croissant soon shall shed its French for patriotism.
The world bursts in springtime splendor at my door,
But in the desert sands, it's bombs that burst—and bodies . . .
And perhaps one day God's truth.

Syria Must Rise

This song if for the Syrian people whom I love.
The ones I have a bond with and the millions I can't touch.
It is especially for all the ones whose souls are now above;
The ones who martyred their bodies for a most noble cause.

Monster is too neutral a word for Bashar. It lacks description.
It lacks truth. The horror and the beast of hell that dwells within
The heart of Assad are beyond the grasp of my beleaguered mind—
The tyrant, like a devil, sheds his soul if he is to survive.

What kind of godless evil is capable of torturing an Angel?
A boy of two hung from a bridge, purple and bloody, as a warning!
What kind of beast; more evil than a monster, beyond words?
The roomful of the innocents, hands bound and shot point blank?

And if a poem were a dagger I could use to gash Bashar Al Assad,
A thousand times I would rejoice. For it is he among the list
Of monsters known to this earth, who drips in the blood of
Citizens and patriots; and he alone can halt the evil now unleashed.

Enough! Enough! I want to shout each day, each time I see
Another bloody face just snuffed. For it too often is an Angel's face,
Most beautiful, children, families tortured to a pulp,
Now gone but still radiant with innocence, and speaking truth.

What is that truth it speaks? It is that guilt and shame
Prevail in Damascus, Aleppo — in the court and body of Assad.
The truth that cannot be veiled away even by the ill-gotten
Powers of the Russians or the Chinese godless interests.

And where is the U.S.? John McCain speaks, but not enough.
Hillary Clinton chastises the Reds. It's not enough!
Kofi Annan resigns and points the blame for naught.
United nations, Turkey, Arab league, it's time, past time, to move!

Oh, how the world stands by in stupor, helpless
To save one Syrian baby from the thug regime.
We read instead about the Desert Rose telling
Vogue fashionistas that she will usher in democracy
And empower the children to make future change.

And then Shahrazad Al Jaffari is outed as the PR beauty
Mastermind who swept the truth aside for the Assad she loves.
Will Columbia University leave spread her welcome mat after this
news
Because she hooked up Barbra Walters with an interview?

Enough, I say again, at yet another lovely face made horrid,
My Face Book screen presents, and the new massacre.
Oh, the beautiful people of the Syrian state, forsaken and yet strong,
When will my President, the first of Arab name, liberate you?

Enough with the excuses, Mr. Barak Obama; children are dying,
And even one of these pure souls killed is already too many.
The citizen of Syria bleeds red blood just as you do.
Human compassion has no citizenship, no boundaries, no price.

The grand Damascus that gave life to our earliest forefathers
Some 10,000 years BC is entitled to protection evermore,
For all its grandiose history and its capital of region and the world.
Or is it right to watch it as it perishes from earth?

Damascus, Arab Capital of Culture, and its 2 million people
Deserve better. Will its 2,000 mosques survive?
Thank God true, noble Syrians still exist for the Free Syrian Army.
There lies the hope, and there will be the victory we seek.

Can the world stand by idle any longer, after seeing the faces
Of the dead up close? Damascus, she that survived the Ottomans
And Alexander the Great, is on the brink of victory over Assad,
But we must cut short the looming bloodbath yet to come.

Another day, another Angel slaughtered, and I cry.
Another day, now the impossibly handsome face
Of a young father appears on my screen with caption "killed."
Another day, another heavy day...since March 2011, 20,000 dead.

Enough! Enough, Bashar Al Assad! Your time is up!
Call back your vicious dogs of hell, the murdering Shadiha thugs.
Shame on the Alawites forever, great shame of the Assads.
Your father Hafez killed enough for the eternal shame of all Assads.

I sing of you, my beautiful Syrian friends, and your martyrs,
I cry for you, the innocent Angelic children killed for naught.
The end of your torment is near, I feel it, and you shall overcome soon,
You, my friends will know the small relief that death will exalt.

Allah, bless the Syrian people!

Syrian Boys

The most famous Syrian boy is Aylan.

Famous. ....Infamous? Neither word will do for what Aylan is.

To be famous suggests too much positivity;

To be infamous connotes perverseness, criminality.

Aylan is neither of those things, yet he is well known.

His image exploded onto the world stage in the most horrid way,

On a beach in Turkey, washed ashore, dead.

Such a child at the heart of tragedy in Syria is not uncommon,

But Aylan had luck on his side to make the splash he did.

Luck?

The beautiful child of 3 was drowned at sea,

So, no. Not luck. Yet his name and face are "viral."

The instrument of fame catapulted little Aylan

Onto the consciousness of millions in mere hours.

The camera and the picture of the precious boy

Washed ashore as if a dead fish, or some plastic debris—

The camera.... and the picture. ....Fame.

That photograph many refuse to view like they reject reality

Portrays a baby boy like a discarded ragdoll.

His little feet still encased in the velcroed tennis shoes

His mother lovingly put on him just before they fled,

Just as the family of four, now only one, prayed

For a safe voyage and breathed silent dreams of freedom

Yet again, his bright red t-shirt, his navy shorts, he lay

Limp and face down on that brown Turkish sand.

That photograph that horrified so many,

Made him known

Even as thousands of other children before him have died

In Syrian towns all over, bombed by crude weapons of horror,

With nary a blink from the cynical world

Let alone the xenophobic Hungary

Whose military corrals them away from freedom trains.

Aylan has become the instrument of God

To bring the self-absorbed world to recognition

Of its humanity, and lack thereof.

The God forsaken Syrian children, their desperate fathers

and mothers too,

Have gone unaided for four years as thousands perish

As millions hunger and flee to lesser miseries

Than a tyrant's bombs or ISIS subjugation.

Aylan has opened one small window of hope,

Of opportunity, with his tragedy and with that picture.

Aylan may yet become the conduit that saves millions;

Or he may be forgotten when one of many

World pantomimes utters another vulgar Trumpism.

May Aylan's life and death not have been in vain.

May Aylan be the hand of God at last,

At long last!

To The Lost Angels

Crumpled minarets!
Shattered domes of mosques.
Dusty streets and alleys;
Everywhere powdered with death.
The rows and stacks of houses,
Of homes pan-caked in rubble.
What do the angels make of this?
The ones lucky enough so far to see still
These sights and their own blood
Accenting the ash-powdered face of horror
Like the whorish rouge of a monstrous
Medusa, whose snaky tentacles are the shabbiha.
Brothers, sisters, playmates — Perish!
Five, or three, or twelve, or newborn
Into Angel-hood in the blink of an eye.
They hide, they run, they cling to
Panicked parents drenched in sweat
And tears caking mud on their
Once glowing, handsome cheeks;
Tasting with dry mouths dirt and gunpowder,
Cement powder from the hellish bombs;
Dodging here and there to outrun
The tentacles and claws of the monster
Called Assad, the coward, root of evil;

Hiding in unknown comfort fortresses
Now self-engulfing prisons yet unseen
By he who wishes not to, but cracked enough
To spew havoc and destruction
Of the Angels and the proud and patriot land,
Whose only sin has been a plea for freedom.
Do not despair sweet Angels,
You shall not be depleted.
For help will surely come, and hope
Must keep your army nourished.
The blind and greedy world must look
Upon your face despite itself.
Bear yet another hundred bullets
Bury yet another hundred of your kin
Be the backbone that will slay the beast.
Syria, it is you and your monster at war!
Syria: so beautiful, so proud — so lost.

To The Syrians Yearning to Be Free

I want to say to you my Syrian friends,
You who are suffering by the millions and dying
By over one-hundred-forty-thousand,
You whose children, entire generations, now
Carry permanent scars and nightmares,
My country, the great U.S. of A., just does not care!

I want to say to you my Syrian friends,
You who have fought three martyred years for freedom
Hoping to be the crowning glory of the Arab Spring,
You who in desperation took aid from whence it came,
Thus could not coalesce behind one hero,
The whole world is forsaking you for that!

I want to say to you my Syrian friends,
You of the once flexible Muslim faith
Who bore so well the progress of modernity,
You who have suffered forty years of tyranny
And compromised with Assad's gang so much,
No hope is to be found even with Arab friends!

I say all this to you my Syrian friends
With a deep sadness and regret about your isolation,
For if the world remains unmoved by children
Annihilated and the million documents of your destruction,
And you cannot strategize a better message, better army,
Then I am sorry, oh so sorry, that my friends are lost.

I'm Gonna Tell God Everything!

"I'm gonna tell God everything!,"
You hear the whimper and the pain;
You hear the sobs, the faith that someone cares —
Ultimately, inevitably, undisputedly —
His tender heart believes: someone must care!

"I'm gonna tell God everything!"
Promises the 3-year-old in dying breath.
He was a Syrian child, another Angel felled
Among so many, who lived a tortured life,
Almost from birth, in that hell-hole the leader dug.

A sweet innocent is born in faith;
His parents will provide for basic needs:
A roof over his head, a mother's milk,
A blanket, hugs and kisses, lullabies,
Even, occasionally, chocolate, honey, dates.

A child of God born in the desert
Is worthy, just as any, of caring and protection.
His worth before the eyes of God as infinite,
His father and his village just as tasked
To do right by him, provide justice, safety.

But not this forsaken child of bright, deep-amber eyes,
Not him. For he was born to strife and horror
That the Beast Bashar cast upon the land.
The minarets and stately domes resembling now
Hellish chambers that sear his tender flesh.

And yet the babe in arms, and then the baby walking,
Saw every form of man-made violation
Of his peace, and of God's laws — And how it hurt!
And how the boy with little language and great tears
Yearned to beg someone to make it stop, please stop!

But no one made it stop.
The gnashing pain piled on. The burning tears unceasing,
The desperate Innocent looked for ones to make it right.
He saw his father cry, his mother die humiliated,
His village torn asunder— and no Judge!

His Angelic protestations fell on deaf ears,
And everywhere he turned he saw fierce flames
Amid the darkness of lost souls.
He turned to Baba hopelessly a wreck;
He looked every direction for a friend.

But no one could be found to stop the evil
That so ruthlessly robbed him of a life.
No pleading, nor a threat, could move the King pretender
To provide peace;... the boy's rag-tag heroes
Martyrs all became; his protectors all dead.

And as he lay in blood and ashes, the precious child,
From yet another Syrian bomb in barrels,
Gave thought to justice in the manner of a child's heart,
That he felt so compelled to reassure them all help would come soon:
"I'm gonna tell God everything!" — and he was gone.

And with those dying words this Angel, may God take his heed,
To every child he left behind, he bestowed hope.
O, precious boy, go up to Heaven now.
Lay in God's arms and comfort, sweetest child,
And tell God everything — Once more.

Ode to Kayla

(Written upon the death of Kayla Mueller at the hands of the terrorists ISIS in Syria)

"Where is the world?"

The children asked her, having heard it from their parents

As it's been said by relatives, neighbors, some adult.

For children, normal children, care little

Of the world, and know it even less.

But normality abandoned these young innocents

Much too long ago, and through their pain,

Their tears from unspeakable loss, they asked.

It was a plea, really: "Please rescue us!"

The world's reply was a deafening silence.

Except for one small voice, one great heart.

And thus Kayla emerged!

She was radiant with love and compassion.

She said, "I am the world!"

And she gave her grain of sand, and grains of wheat,

That to one child became the world.

She, too, shed bitter tears in solidarity,

And she, too, tried to shake the world awake.

She left the American desert where she was an oasis

To ride the Syrian desert of despair.

Amid the bullets and the barrel bombs,

She gave her all to every child in need,

Braving the wrath of ISIS the monster
And the monster Assad just the same.
The jaded world stood by as she was caged
By depraved demons. And then she was no more.
Where is the world today, Oh, Kayla of the sky?
For the children suffer still;
And you hold the hand of God.

Section 6

To Stave or
to Hold

Transitions and Quizzes

You have a life to live, so know the basics.

Nothing is constant except change, transitions.

They become the mystery of all the ages.

They come, some slow, some so much faster.

I am standing on the edge, transition waiting,

Wondering, fearing perhaps, but joyful too,

Knowing that my life's lessons guide my journey still,

Knowing that there is no fulfillment in comfort.

It is the road, the traveled one and the one not taken,

That makes the journey a wonder and rewards,

So I embrace the change and the transition.

Looking back my day of birth was much more meaningful to mom

Then followed a parade of letting go:

Separation on the day of the first classroom,

And the change in holding teacher's hand;

The day of losing an uncle to gunfire,

Or grandma to heart failure though I left before,

Those were transitions too.

Like moving day in childhood to new country,

Like acting on my puppy love, then love love

The ache of blind steps and joy of ever present hope;

Like seeking higher knowledge or a public voice,

Every transition just as courageous and bright,

So change is not an end. It is also rebirth.

Every career and every teacher celebrates it,

For it is the constant that makes a country or a woman great.

It is the ever-present yearning that rejuvenates each heart.

Like every test a teacher gives, it can be mastered,

With an attitude of can-do and preparing day to day.

Don't fear the pop quiz; trust your dedication.

Don't fear transitions; embrace them and rejoice!

Profound Pedant

He likes to tell me he's profound,
That all his thoughts are complex.
He claims his words misunderstood
That few appreciate what's good.

He frowns upon seekers of ease
In too much contemporary lit.;
That they are lazy, dense, obtuse;
That they lack insight of the muse.

Today he read his poems aloud
To a crowd by invitation only.
Devotees nodded, smiled, and murmured;
They shook hands, praised him, endured.

His face beamed in full contentment
Until overhearing a pair of complaints —
That his themes were venal, contrary;
Syntax obscure, mystique unnecessary.

He rang me up at ten past midnight,
After his wine and cheese soiree.
He held my ear hostage quite a while,
Blasting the pair of critics with bile.

What to say to my preening complainer,
His laments so predictably lame —
I nodded and hemmed in bored trance,
Rolling my eyes to such a pedant dance.

Second Wife Desserts

You are the second wife, and maybe he to you.
The first one is long gone and has new life.
When he met you he prayed for better luck
He looked into your starry eyes and heart
And he saw hope and love, or so he thought,
So he braved marriage for a second time.

He gathered family and courage round
And introduced them all to you, a precious find.
You put on your best face and swore
You loved him; took his mother in your arms.
So, too, his siblings, one by one your own;
You even vowed to love his son the more.

But you carried a secret in your breast.
It was a plan to take total control.
You never shared with him the depths
Of all your weaknesses, jealousy the worst.
There was pathology and narcissism there,
Plus insecurity so deep it trumped the church.
One could say he was rash or that you pushed him,
But soon a full-flair wedding spectacle arose.

True love builds up; never tears down.

No love is true nor pure when it procures in chains.

You quickly banished the first wife from sight;

After the wedding, his first son was, too, eschewed.

In time, after your son was born, his mother followed,

Jettisoned because she nurtured his first-born.

Lists of petty offences grew from week to day,

And every inconvenient loved one, no matter

Favorite sister or best friend, became unloved.

And now the man who thought he found his family and happiness

At last, can't say how much he gained or lost of either or of both.

Shower in Pashawar

I want to shower in Pashawar;
I want to swim in Berlin,
Partake of the beauty that's in every corner
Of the grand cities of my dreams.

I want to chow in Moscow
I want to work in New York
Revel in all of the marvels
Whether by foot, by train, or by fork.

I want to shiver in Rhine the river
I want to possess in the Suez
Thrill in the heights of the Alps
And with bathers at San Luis Pass.

These are the yearnings I have for the world
To see it, and touch it, and taste
To make it a part of my blood
As the darn thing's captured my mind.

Free Me

I don't remember
How my freedom felt
Before I was entrapped
In this casement of flesh
That binds me like heavy, rusty chains.
I remember only vaguely
The freedom and the joy
Of my terrestrial peak
In perfect skin so fleeting
Like just another dream.
I yearn to shed these chains —
The flesh, the bone, the nagging
Organs and the tearing nerves,
Punishment enough to be weighted
Down with earthy casing in painful decline.
The sinews and the joints, the blood,
Do war for months on end
With brave invaders, stealthy,
Vicious, microscopic evil,
Each ache another bar
To freedom, now a stranger.
I don't remember freedom
Nor the truth;
Free me again
And let me see —
Free me again!

The Turning of Leaves

The golden leaves are falling
I see them through my window,
My morning bright-lit window,
That lets in the sound of chirping sparrows.
This Houston December seems more
Apropos to Snow White and squirrels
Than white snow for Santa Claus,
But a welcome chill and breeze
Stir the still leafy lithe giants,
The pecans in the semi tropic,
Desperate imitation of New England's turning
Of the leaves — golden in the white
Light of morning — and now falling,
Now flying to clumsy landings on the green,
Still green, grass. Now swimming
In the air like tadpoles in a hurry,
Now racing past the squirrels on the tree,
Racing their peers like sperm desperate
To reach the glory of fertility.
Another second of a northern rustle.
Another shower of autumn's confetti,
Past Clara's blooming red hibiscuses
To the cheering of the crows 100 feet above;
And a few months hence each leaf
A winner having fertilized the spring.

Big City Neighbors

They came to help him die.
It's been days or maybe weeks,
The gray haired couple
Appeared on his front porch.
The gray house I see from my lawn
Whose gray porch only sported
A man and his best friend before
The motions of a man and loyal dog,
My neighbor not so neighborly
And me less so, only exchanging
Names and glances or a timid wave,
Is perishing alone in his gray house
Whose frowning color so prevails
With triumphant glow of Montrose
Designer approved, but in the toil of death
Can't hide its colorless essence.
 I Think they're kin, parents perhaps,
Too shy, too circumscribed, to simply ask
And make a friendly inquiry as to my neighbor
And his health – guessing instead by his stationary
SUV, the strange new car bearing Arkansas plates,
The IV fluid holder, discreet but visible
Through the screen, in my evening walk –
Signs telling tales. In a moment of reflection,

Upon a glimpse of a kind woman's white hair
Watching the vigil she and her husband keep,
I shed a tear, as it occurs to me
These elder frail folks won't leave
Until their son is buried right.

End of Time

I was watching CNN, channel 625
The kids were watching other things
Channel 500, channel 210, 06, 400, 825
And of 300 million yearning
To be understood few watched
The news telling of growing brood of disunity
The narrow and the broad minds
Miles apart
And every other mind so close and spanning
But somehow each a portal of its own
And walled apart even from neighbors
So when the epidemic came
And then the plagues had to be fought
I reached out in desperation and managed in a word
To a few kids and a few kin
And rejoiced when I heard others did the same
And formed a circle of their own
But looking back each circle
Reached a wall and moved no more
And like the 1000 channels
There grew a 1000 fronts
Too few able to merge the walls
In time to stave the flood.
And so it was when nearing
End of time

Haiku

Fall, Spring —
The multitudes thrive
By your smile.

Social Security

They come. Sporadically, they come.
Timidly resolute to plead their case,
Sometimes each sunny morning,
Their home country's paper wealth
Having vanished upon their university admission.
Like supplicants, they come. The foreign.
Their faces framing wide-eyes, hopeful,
Ever hopeful; and beautiful in their agony,
Beautiful in their old-world dignity
And in the vulnerability of pleading in restraint;
Requesting simple favors, a hearing. A job.
Having heard somehow there's a corner
Of hope here, and having been forewarned
That the door has closed. And yet...
It closed just yesterday. Perhaps
It's still ajar. They ask, quivering
Youthful lips smiling, hoping, pleading.
They ask the man, assuming power,
Not knowing, not caring, he has none but this
Small command of paper pieces.
The early ones, the lucky ones,
They hold the note, in trembling clutch of triumph
Chin Heavenward in gratitude for small miracles —
The Sudanese, the Venezuelans, Chads, Lebanese —

That moment greedily tucking their prize,

The letter like a passport, for permission

To work. Beyond the rigors of a science

Lab lie greater rigors for a plate of food;

And so they come. Again; all other doors

Having been locked. They whisper secretly his name

Only to one close friend, the desperate one.

The "nice man" will understand the need,

The floating wide-eyes;

He'll make one more exception,

They pray;

The lonely, hopeful foreigners amid great American

Academic castles — while navigating all the forms

Of border-crossings and protectionism.

And the man trains the gate-keeper yet again

Because he must avert the discomfort of the "No"

And enforce the trifling rules to the hungry.

Nightmare Postmodern

I was enticed to call you friend
When you took me to the feast
At your estate that brackish night
Of sordid music and disarrayed rooms
To my surprise. It was more crowded
Than you said, and cold
When you left me with strangers
Like an abandoned child
Whose parents have found new joys.
And my head spun from the stares
And the stench of burning sweets.
There were bubbling, noisy
Pecan pies in the ovens,
The monstrous ovens of dark
Hotel kitchens, or like those kitchens,
But it was yours.
I knew the choking aroma
As I looked frantic through windows
Of the stainless steel doors.
They bubbled dull-flat-gold and huge and sour;
And spilled over, overcooking,
Like the hideous rocky lips
Of a volcano, gold and black,
The meats bubbled under;

While I ran to your arms

That disappeared, always,

Disappeared at my approach

Or turned to disappointment

And faces I don't know,

Who question

Everything I have, my arms,

My voiceless agony

To hear you behind every door

And not find you; frantic

Through the groaning house and kitchen

Filled with gross buffets

And painted relatives in plastic joy

But for the burning sweets,

And you gone.

Offerings Burning

Your brown feet are amazing,
so let me help them stay;
make these the finest cottons
their snuggle every day.

And though your crotch and privates
I much prefer in hand,
I've spun a warm snug draper
as for rich contraband.

How fast I lose my senses
thinking of your silk breast,
but wear this undervestment;
I'll give passion a rest.

A Mexican song echoes
wishes she were cigar
so that he could alight her
and his mouth could get that far.

Just so I have no choice
for no cigarette are you,
so I live in each these garments
for your soul; your sweat; for you.

Lost Answers

It was eleven o'clock that Monday night.
I was wrapping Christmas gifts in brown
Paper bags deconstructed to serve
The soon-to-be air mailed sweets to you,
My sister in another state, so far.

That Monday night it was the coldest yet
In some ten years and my hands white
And blue with unnimbling fingers
Fought the brown brittle parchment, thick
Enough to hold heavy apples and canned beans,
To write lovingly your name and state.

How my brown eyes strained past the gray
Matter of my brain and of the distances
To absorb the longed for, long longed for
Happiness a simple package, no bigger
Than a shoe box, brings in its rumpled brown.

The rain outside fell hard and beat loudly
My window like a squadron of bugs slamming
Their shellacked bodies against the invisible
Killer wall of a speeding night car. And I remembered
Then you flew like a blind Texas valley cricket
Into a headlight you thought would bring relief.

1990 New West

Desperate, pathetic metaphors.

Contrived!

To demonstrate a skill,

To equal art.

The art of the bourgeoisie;

For the bourgeois critics,

Each one just as pathetic,

Showing off his and her hand me down

Checklists of the newest fads,

To feed the fellows, in metaphor,

To impress the plastic souls that guard,

That pass for multitudes,

The multitudes be damned!

Desperate allusion!

To the lofty old —

Like Plato — he was right

About our blindness

And the shadows in the cave.

You have doubts.

Of course!

Plato was a shadow

Like you and me,

For what do you know of brown?

Or the American democratic stamp?

You push the imbeciles

For laws confusing

Symbols for the truth — the flag.

Contrived metaphor.

Desperate personification.

For a woman is as much as the universe;

And just as great,

Scares you to red panic.

"Heresy," you shout in plastic motions,

Stirring the zombie multitude

And desperate call up

For cure, for refuge

Dozens of anesthetic metaphors.

Of Loves and Dogs

When I was just a child,
I saw two country dogs in full abandon,
As they do.
Chased apart by boys with stones
Instead they locked in flesh.
And through their panic and thwarted flight
Each beast in opposite, desperate to run,
Scurried into the woods
In crab-like motion, yelping.

I thought, "Have dogs no shame?"
For it was such a public act
In quite a sunny day;
And they hid not their passion
Nor their lust—
Like humans must, or do—
And they knew not the threat
Of youths with stones.

Yet as I stared in youthful judgment
I was fascinated, too.
And as a child of eight I hoped,
Without the words,
With lots of luck and skill,
One day I'd know such passion
As the dogs. . .

Soul

What is there to explore to make you whole?
A fear, a laugh, a green envy, a red tear?
The ugliness of dark corners and forced-shut eyes
Does not always go away when a friend arrives.
The throbbing of ignorance is not so dim
When those you bring are in their drown.
Everyone goes to the pinks and the gauzy
Not the hardness of the deeper purple;
The heat of the throbbing red, the raw green.
Friends are yours at instants, moments—
Don't fool you or them with easy comforts
That come effortlessly or fleetingly though timely.
There is no glory in pretend love, mirage embrace.
The whole will not be fooled. It will be pained.
The ceaseless noise of crashing rocks and waters
Is just a mild reminder that love wants out,
That teeming spirits must resist the binds.

Lost Treasures

Your gift is temporary
I guess three, maybe four
More years
Of blooming bliss are yours
It may have been a loan
For just so long
To do to men those things
That make us foolish
All to your delight
But temporarily
It will all be
You'll see
When that rose leaves your cheek
That diamond shuns your eye
That gold deserts your skin
Like they did me
You'll understand
And when you love
The splendors of the gift
That temporary gift
Will you not shed a tear
For this spurned offering
The treasures that I've built
Wise as a sage I guess

J.C. Salazar

Will get me through or us
Further than dewy youth
My now lost treasure
Like yours too shall be soon.

Links Missing

A flooding happens.
It is orange like that of tangerines,
Unpleasantly warm, sticky.
It is the knowledge of lost hope,
Or unmaterialized unions,
Like the finger of Adam
Failing forever to touch God.
A deluge roars in from the cobwebs
Of the white bedroom
And the brown-black of the brain
To shriek like a million crows
The lament of loveliness unrealized,
And to cut you with the blankness
Of the sought-for image of love,
Never having been defined.
The torrent of sea-tears
Smudges all the edges of the heart
Like a shower hot upon the face
Makes chaos of the maybellined eyes
Of the teenage streetwalker
In Chelsea.
Burn, sticky tangerine waters
That never quench a thirst,
For searching endlessly

For new warm mouths,

Becoming warmer still,

And leaving red-glow orange muck behind.

Burn, like you burn my eyes.

Burn to white.

September Joy

I was born in the month of September,
my favorite time of pure winds;
when life begins again
more powerful than spring —
alike in ivy-covered walls
and those withstanding graffiti —
when expectant
men and women
hold their impregnated pages,
releasing facts and truths
and glimpses of forever;
in the cool breezes
for just such a cacophony,
not mistaking blazing leaves for death.

September birthing
doubly elevates these eyes
with breezy welcome to the flesh
and classroom camaraderie to the soul.
The verdure missing in its slopes
opens more vivid panorama
through such parts;
you vainly wait for April
the deceiver,

J.C. Salazar

promising fleeting gardens pure and strong,

grasping for birthing promises

too soon destroyed

while truer friend September goes ignored.

I was born in the month of September

and good company keep I for that.

They are wisdom and sight and a measure of joy

like the ninth month's breezes report.

Ditties?

A ditty
A poem
A song
Beckon you upward,
Kill the yawn.

Have you a plume
You can dip in a well
And point to a pristine birth?

Or trace on the page
Your Cervantes-made line
For a scroll to nurture
Your soul?

Dime Store Prophets

You come calling for my child,
Or my friend or sister sweet.
Are you here to bring good tidings
Or your carnal yens to feed?

Be forewarned I love them all,
Young or old, and blood or not,
And they stumble in the darkness
That the blinding sun provides.

They go forth in all good faith
To a sure and stable rest.
And your gilded words deter them
From their humble rosy paths.

Take your gaudy faux-silk mantles
And your wiseness parroted,
Don't distract with your banality;
You give nothing, only take.

You can brag about your travels
And your college ivy prize,
And pretend that you are high,
Ride the praise of foreign tongues.

Too polite to ask newcomer
For credential or its proof;
They don't know the proper question:
"Are you a builder or a sham?"

I know you're a hanger on,
Not a builder of things strong;
And your swathed naive disguise
Lures a lamb to quench your lust.

They can't see that you've not built
A home or even a house.
Have you laid a brick for children,
Buttressed towers for communes?

Your gold's borrowed from sweet kin,
Half investment, mostly love.
And your academy tool?—
Is sore in need of whetstone.

You're a user-up of life,
Never bothering to build;
All your forces, fancy manner,
Have been counterfeit, clichés.

Keep away from these my dear ones.
Keep your flimsy rides and fancies.
Their good honest toil of sweat
Serves them well; past your mirage.

Soon your creditors will out,
And your lies will daze my kin.
They will know too late your voids,
You built not a single thing.

You must crash and hurt and yelp
Like in fates of parasites;
You will learn your pain in ten-fold
Too late to restore my lambs.

You will learn that truth of lusting,
The high price of good destroyed.

Sons of Bitches

They killed Claudia!
Claudia Patricia Gomez Gonzalez.
Remember her name.
The sons of bitches killed her.
John Kelly, Jeff Sessions,
You sons of bitches.
How could a man with a soul as black
As yours ever become
A four-star general?
Someone who aids and abets
Thugs that give poorly trained would-be cops
License to kill?
Someone who rips children, infants
From the arms of their mothers?
Someone who responds to accusations of "inhumane"
With "the children will be taken care of —
Or whatever."?
That is a son of a bitch.
Or "whatever"?
I may be violating the Worthsworthian rule,
Not relating an emotion recollected in tranquility.
But I am not tranquil.
I cannot be.
Because the world is in the hands of tyrants and despots.

Tyrants must be called out;

Despots must be called what they are.

And they must be stopped.

No one should be tranquil when tyrants and despots rule.

The sons of bitches killed Claudia.

Claudia. Twenty years old. Beautiful, indigenous;

Grand in her Sunday best, sweet and lovely;

Courageous and braving all hazards

To provide for her family —

Beause of love, because of the accident

Of her birth in a county condemned

To be perpetually raped

By sons of bitches.

The United States of America

Is at the height of its disuniting

All its citizens and all the world,

To satisfy the whims of sons of bitches

And the bigotry of sons of bitches

Who would just as soon choose

To live in a Nazi Third Reich

Than in a multicultural society

Where the lofty words of the constitution

Reach fruition,

That all men are equal;

Because we are, indeed, created equal.

So they destroy the fabric

That made America great despite its flaws;
They tear apart what's left of decency.
They kill.
They shoot a young woman in the head
For no other reason than her needs.
Claudia was her name.
Claudia Patricia Gomez Gonzalez.
Remember her name.
They killed her,
The sons of bitches.

J.C. Salazar

The author was born in the
village of Ramirez, a farming
community outside the town of
General Teran, in the valley of
Monterrey (Mexico). He grew
up in Houston in the barrio
neighborhood known as Second Ward, where he graduated
from Austin High School and eventually earned a BA, MS,
and MA from UH and UH-Clear Lake. After a career as an
English teacher at both his alma mater high school and
Houston community college, J.C. took early retirement
and began to write in earnest, taking his previous hobby
to new levels and publishing his debut novel, "Of Dreams
& Thorns," in February, 2017. "states of unitedness" is his
poetry collection, which includes poems as old as forty
years. J.C. has not followed the traditional route of poets
who perform at public readings, but he hopes readers of
poetry will find helpful truths in his verses.

www.ingramcontent.com/pod-product-compliance
Lightning Source LLC
Chambersburg PA
CBHW030104070426
42448CB00037B/966